Heroes

Heroes

(Le Vent des Peupliers)

GÉRALD SIBLEYRAS

TRANSLATED BY TOM STOPPARD

Grove Press
New York

Library of Congress Cataloging-in-Publication Data

Sibleyras, Gérald.
    [Vent des peupliers. English]
    Heroes = Le vent des peupliers / Gerald Sibleyras ; translated by Tom Stoppard.
        p. cm.
    Originally published: London : Faber and Faber, 2005.
    ISBN-10: 0-8021-4287-7
    ISBN-13: 978-0-8021-4287-0
    I. Stoppard, Tom. II. Title. III. Title: Vent des peupliers.
    PQ2719.I25V4613 2006
    842'.92—dc22

                                                                2006049509

Grove Press
an imprint of Grove/Atlantic, Inc.
841 Broadway
New York, NY 10003

Distributed by Publishers Group West

www.groveatlantic.com

07 08 09 10 11 12   10 9 8 7 6 5 4 3 2 1

Heroes in this translation was first performed at Wydham's Theatre, London, on October 7, 2005, presented by David Pugh, Dafydd Rogers and the Shubert Organisation. The cast was as follows:

HENRI Richard Griffiths
GUSTAVE John Hurt
PHILIPPE Ken Stott

Director Thea Sharrock
Designer Rob Jones
Lighting Designer Howard Harrison
Projection Designer Jon Driscoll
Sound Designers Simon Baker and Alan Lugger
Music Steve Parry
Costume Supervisor Jack Galloway
Assistant Director Claire Lovett

CHARACTERS

PHILIPPE

GUSTAVE   } veterans, residents in an old soldiers' home

HENRI

SCENE I

A terrace. The only ornamental object is a stone statue of a dog. Three men are seated. PHILIPPE is reading a newspaper. GUSTAVE stares into the distance. The steadiness of his gaze is similar to the dog's. HENRI has his leg stretched out, a walking stick near him, a book on his lap.

HENRI   I love the month of August.

GUSTAVE   I knew it couldn't last. The world was at peace, and you had to share with us your passion for the month of August.

PHILIPPE   Don't you like the month of August?

GUSTAVE   No. I hate the month of August. If months were days of the week, August would be Sunday . . . a pointless, paltry affair.

HENRI   But heralding the lovely colours of autumn.

GUSTAVE   Don't talk to me about autumn. September and October are living death. November is the funeral . . . December is the stupidest month of the lot—Christmas! January and February you think are never going to end . . . March and April can't make up their minds . . . Then—God help us—here come May, June, July . . .

PHILIPPE   It's a bugger.

HENRI   I ran into Sister Madeleine after breakfast. Chassagne's having his birthday party tonight.

GUSTAVE   Is there to be no end to this mania for celebrating birthdays? This is a home for veterans, not a day nursery.

PHILIPPE   I agree, it's quite unbearable.

GUSTAVE   She's obsessed, that Madeleine, she's mad for celebrating everything!

I

PHILIPPE   I'm dreading this New Year's.

HENRI   Why?

PHILIPPE   1960! A new decade! She'll outdo herself.

GUSTAVE   That's true, she must have been waiting ten years for this moment.

HENRI   Meanwhile, it's Chassagne's birthday.

PHILIPPE   Have you noticed there's never two birthdays on the same day?

HENRI   No.

PHILIPPE   And you know why? Because Sister Madeleine won't have it. I suspect she doles out the drugs according to your date of birth—if your birthday falls on a free day, you live; if not . . .

HENRI   If not what?

PHILIPPE   You remember Morot, Captain Morot?—his birthday was February 12th, same as mine. He died six weeks after he arrived. It was him or me. That was a close shave.

HENRI   He was at death's door when he got here.

PHILIPPE   No, no, Sister Madeleine got rid of him, trust me, because of his birthday. She, as it were, chose me.

GUSTAVE   Not that you're in the pink yourself.

PHILIPPE   She chose me, all the same.

HENRI   Well anyway, she's asked me—with your help, she made a point of that—to compose a little couplet in honour of Lieutenant Chassagne.

PHILIPPE   How long has he been here?

HENRI   Ages.

GUSTAVE   What's he like?

HENRI   Big.

GUSTAVE   How big?

HENRI   He's huge . . . almost incalculable.

PHILIPPE   You must have noticed him. He has a permanent blissful smile and great difficulty in finishing a sentence . . . also starting one. A child at heart, you might say.

HENRI   A gigantic baby.

GUSTAVE   No, I haven't seen him. You know me, I never leave my room, except to come to our terrace and bore myself with your company. Then I have my tepid soup and go to bed . . . There's so many lunatics around.

PHILIPPE   Why is it we've been given the honour of composing a little couplet for Lieutenant Chassagne?

HENRI   Because he holds us in high esteem, I had it from Sister Madeleine.

GUSTAVE   He can't hold *me* in high esteem. I've never said a word to him.

PHILIPPE   That's what must have impressed him.

HENRI   Any ideas for a little couplet?

PHILIPPE   . . . No. (*going back to his newspaper*) How about you, Gustave?

GUSTAVE   I don't even know the man.

HENRI Well, but Madeleine asked us to do it . . . so let's . . .

There is a silence, during which Philippe and Gustave quite obviously give the matter no thought.

HENRI (*cont.*) It means a lot to Chassagne . . . His eighty-fifth birthday. A little quatrain, a mere squib . . . that rhymes . . . What rhymes with "agne"?

GUSTAVE Pffft . . . Dunno.

HENRI I have the impression you don't care.

PHILIPPE Why should we care?

HENRI Well, that's not very nice . . . and Sister Madeleine's going to be very disappointed.

PHILIPPE No, it's not very nice, but it's you she asked, and it's you she'll hold responsible.

HENRI Right—fine—I'll sort something out myself. (*to himself to the rhythm of* "La Mer") "Chassagne! . . . da-da-dum . . . da-da . . ."

PHILIPPE It's funny how afraid you are of Sister Madeleine.

HENRI I'm not afraid. I'm just trying to be nice.

PHILIPPE You're scared stiff.

HENRI No I'm not.

PHILIPPE Anyway, I don't blame you, she's terrifying.

HENRI "Chassagne! at the sound of your name!—my heart . . ."

PHILIPPE With Madeleine it's like with wild animals, if you let her see you're afraid, she goes for you. Your mistake is letting her see you're petrified.

4

HENRI "Chassagne! let me count the ways . . ."

PHILIPPE You know that chap Mercier . . . ?

GUSTAVE Who?

PHILIPPE Major Mercier.

GUSTAVE What about him?

PHILIPPE He nearly came to blows with her.

GUSTAVE I biffed her one myself.

HENRI You biffed her?

PHILIPPE She had it coming.

HENRI Why?

GUSTAVE No reason. I bumped into her one day and sensing she was off guard, I took my chance and biffed her one . . . since then there's been a distinct coolness between us.

HENRI . . . "The name of Lieutenant Chassagne
Still sounds o'er the fields of Champagne . . ."
Not too bad for a start. What do you think?

PHILIPPE I don't think anything. I'm waiting to see how it comes out before I offer an opinion.

HENRI Gustave? "Chassagne . . . Champagne" . . . ?

GUSTAVE (*after a beat*) "He's colossal, he's immense,
A man of action, a man of sense,
There's no one like Chassagne,
But most of all, he's our friend."

The other two are stunned for a moment.

HENRI That's perfect— it's awfully good—very well done!

GUSTAVE   It's a gift.

HENRI   I'll write it out.

He takes out a notebook and discovers a letter in his pocket.

PHILIPPE   Sister Madeleine is going to be thrilled.

GUSTAVE   Pity.

HENRI   Oh—she gave me your post to give you.

Philippe looks at the envelope and gives it to Gustave.

GUSTAVE (*taking the post*)   Thank you.

HENRI   I can't understand why you give Gustave your post.

PHILIPPE   Why?

HENRI   Well, it's not very nice to the people who take the trouble to write to you.

PHILIPPE   It's my sister. I'm bored with her. We've been writing the same things to each other for ten years. Gustave is welcome.

Gustave chuckles as he reads. Henri looks over his shoulder but Gustave hides the letter, with a look of disapproval.

GUSTAVE (*to Philippe*)   He really is a pain in the arse, your cousin Pierre, isn't he? Wait till I tell him what I think of him.

HENRI   You mean you reply?

GUSTAVE   It's the least one can do.

HENRI   Don't they suspect?

GUSTAVE   They were slightly disconcerted at the beginning when I kept getting everybody in the family mixed up. What's more, I sign myself "Gustave," so they probably think he's sustained a heavy blow to the head . . . which, on the other hand, isn't so far from the truth.

HENRI   I didn't know you replied.

Philippe has closed his eyes. His arms drop. He has passed out.

HENRI (*cont.*)   Philippe's passed out again.

GUSTAVE   Not again!

HENRI   It's his bit of shrapnel up to it's old tricks again . . . Philippe . . . Philippe . . .

GUSTAVE   He's always passing out, it's very odd.

HENRI   Ah, he's coming round.

PHILIPPE (*still out*)   We'll take them from the rear, captain . . . take them from the rear . . .

HENRI   That's it—you'll take them from the rear.

GUSTAVE   And always saying the same thing when he's coming round . . . You have to admit it's odd. Are you feeling better, Philippe?

PHILIPPE   I'm fine, thank you . . . sorry . . . dizzy spell. They seem to be getting more frequent, do you think?

Gustave and Henri are slightly embarrassed.

HENRI   No.

GUSTAVE   I hadn't noticed . . .

HENRI   By the way

PHILIPPE   What?

HENRI   That other terrace—the one overlooking the park in front—it's going to be dug up soon, did you know?

PHILIPPE   No.

HENRI   There's a notice on the board—didn't you see it?

PHILIPPE   I never saw any notice.

HENRI   Yes, they're going to redo all the paving. Good thing, too. It's covered in moss. Dangerous stuff, moss, slippery.

GUSTAVE   It's all the same to me, I never go there—too crowded.

HENRI   That's my point. I'm afraid the troops are going to fall back on this one.

PHILIPPE   This one what?

HENRI   Terrace.

GUSTAVE   Which?

HENRI   This one here.

PHILIPPE   Ours?

HENRI   Yes. Ours. This terrace.

PHILIPPE   What, you mean they're going to come over to our terrace here.

HENRI   Well done! It's simple mechanics. If you do away with the big terrace at the front, you have a displacement to the little one at the back , , ,

Gustave and Philippe are upset.

GUSTAVE   Now you tell us!

HENRI   You only had to look at the noticeboard.

PHILIPPE   This terrace is our terrace. It's private!

HENRI   (*dubiously*)   Well, to be strictly legal . . .

GUSTAVE I'm telling you, if we don't do something, those disgusting old tramps'll be grabbing our chairs to slurp their mugs of cocoa.

PHILIPPE We have to defend the position.

HENRI (*ironically*) Barbed wire, sandbags, trenches, it'll be like the old days.

PHILIPPE When does this work begin, do you know?

HENRI Before summer's over, I assume.

PHILIPPE They can attack on two fronts.

GUSTAVE We should seal off this approach here and defend that one there.

PHILIPPE Three lines of barbed wire. Blockade of sandbags. Two machine guns deployed there and there to set up a crossfire to spray the whole grounds. Anyone who sticks his head out is dead meat.

GUSTAVE No, too defensive! No, what would do the job better is a 75 field gun over there, only higher up.

HENRI Right! With the three of us, and a good supply of ammo and some hand grenades, we can hold this position to the end of September, mid-October maybe.

PHILIPPE That would do. They'd have to postpone to next year.

GUSTAVE You have to earn the right to this terrace, it's not open house. Look at that view! It's superb!

HENRI You mean the cemetery?

GUSTAVE No, higher up.

HENRI   Those trees in the distance?

PHILIPPE   Trees! They're poplars, Henri!

GUSTAVE   Can you see the poplars?

HENRI   Yes . . . yes . . .

GUSTAVE   They're moving!

HENRI   So they are . . . they're moving.

Gustave and Henri stare at the horizon. Henri sits down again.

GUSTAVE   Constantly shaken by the wind, while down here, not a breath. For the six months I've been here, I've been watching the tops of the poplars swaying in the wind. It's a sort of perpetual motion.

PHILIPPE   A beautiful sight to see . . .

HENRI   (*casting a quick glance*)   Mmmm . . . They're a bit far away for me.

PHILIPPE   A row of distant poplars swaying in the wind . . .

GUSTAVE   And here, not a breath.

HENRI   You're making me seasick.

GUSTAVE   They're so stately, poplars . . . but supple, bending before the wind.

PHILIPPE   Unlike us.

GUSTAVE   (*to Henri*)   You don't give a toss, do you?

HENRI   Oh, yes, they're lovely, sublime. Now about tonight, dinner's at seven.

PHILIPPE   Tonight?

HENRI Chassagne. It won't take long—a toast, a poem and off to bed, everybody happy.

GUSTAVE You're obsessed with Chassagne, aren't you? Chassagne, Chassagne, Chassagne!

HENRI Surely one may now and again take part in the primitive social life of this barracks?

GUSTAVE What's this fellow to us when all's said and done? You've got your little poem—fine—now shut up about him.

HENRI Right! You're being disagreeable now. I'll leave you to it.

GUSTAVE Now you're being pompous.

HENRI Not at all, I'm leaving you to your poplars.

PHILIPPE We've got nothing against him, Henri, it's only . . .

HENRI You're right, to hell with him . . . Poor devil, on his way out, getting a kick out of his eighty-fifth birthday party . . . I'm awfully sorry, I should have realised it's all sadly humdrum for elevated minds like yours.

GUSTAVE You're being a bit touchy, Henri.

PHILIPPE He's right, Henri—don't take it so hard.

HENRI No, I'm off, you're getting on my nerves.

Henri sets off, leaning on his stick.

PHILIPPE Henri!

Henri exits.

GUSTAVE He gets into these states for no reason at all.

PHILIPPE   He's really upset.

GUSTAVE   And touchy with it.

PHILIPPE   (*pause*)   Are you coming to this birthday party?

GUSTAVE   Of course.

BLACKOUT

SCENE 2

Philippe and Gustave.

PHILIPPE   Your poem was a triumph. He was overwhelmed.

GUSTAVE   Real tears!

PHILIPPE   Sister Madeleine was beside herself. After this she'll be coming to you for every birthday.

GUSTAVE   I could kill Henri for telling her it was me who came up with it.

PHILIPPE   Do you think he'll be coming today?

GUSTAVE   Henri? Oh, yes.

PHILIPPE   We were a bit hard on him.

GUSTAVE   Don't worry, he'll show up any moment.

PHILIPPE   Perhaps he's on the other terrace.

GUSTAVE   No, he's frightened of moss! Besides, he likes being with us. He's happy here. It's the only thing I've got against him.

PHILIPPE   He's been here twenty-five years, it's the momentum.

GUSTAVE No, I don't think so, it's his nature. He's a born enthusiast, he's stuck with it. When he's dead he'll be an enthusiastic corpse.

PHILIPPE I'm rather fond of him.

GUSTAVE So am I. It's him who doesn't like me . . . He's jealous.

PHILIPPE Of what?

GUSTAVE Me reading your post.

PHILIPPE . . . Yes, possibly . . .

GUSTAVE And then you two have known each other for ten years, and I showed up six months ago. You were a threesome, now suddenly we're a quartet, it's hard for him to accept that.

PHILIPPE A quartet?

GUSTAVE I was counting the dog.

Henri enters.

PHILIPPE Aaah!

GUSTAVE Ah, Henri.

PHILIPPE We were just wondering where you were.

HENRI Gentlemen, I've made a sensational discovery.

GUSTAVE (*quietly to Philippe*) An enthusiast . . .

PHILIPPE Well, tell us what it is.

HENRI For some time, as you know, it's been my custom to do a circuit of the grounds, following the boundary wall . . . my daily constitutional. Well, yesterday, after I left you to your poplar trees, I took my courage in both hands and launched a surprise attack on the cemetery—which, once I'd traversed it, allowed me to scout out the little village that adjoins the sanatorium. And that little village, gentlemen, conceals a real treasure.

PHILIPPE What's that?

GUSTAVE (*pretending enthusiasm*) Oh, indeed, tell us everything.

HENRI A school for young girls!

GUSTAVE Sensational!

PHILIPPE A school for young girls is mainly interesting for the young girls inside the school. Did you see any?

HENRI As plain as I see you. I must have got there just as it was time for their walk.

GUSTAVE I had no idea girls were walked.

HENRI Each one lovelier than the one before. Fresh as daisies, smiling faces . . . slim ankles . . . they were a sight.

GUSTAVE Many of them?

HENRI They were all around me, like starlings, bursting into the alley from a side-door. I was literally surrounded. They immediately showed the most profound respect for my leg and melted my heart with their shy sympathetic smiles . . . At first I remained very soldier-hero-proud-of-his-sacrifice, then I spotted the young woman in charge.

PHILIPPE What was she like?

HENRI A rose. She smiled at me from under her lowered lashes. I lost my self-possession, what was left of it. Then all of a sudden they'd vanished, leaving me standing there on my leg and a half, helpless to follow them.

PHILIPPE How old are these young girls?

HENRI Oh . . . twelve, thirteen.

GUSTAVE That's about right for someone of your age, an interest in twelve year old girls.

PHILIPPE Be careful all the same, Henri, it might look fishy, limping along after a bunch of schoolgirls.

GUSTAVE This rose of yours, describe her.

HENRI Like a flower.

PHILIPPE Apart from that.

HENRI A lily, rather . . . tall . . . lissom . . . long-limbed . . .

GUSTAVE Ah—see, you're a poet, too.

HENRI You have to admit it's a turn-up. I didn't even know there was a school for young girls half a mile away.

GUSTAVE Nor me.

HENRI Well, of course you didn't, you never go out.

GUSTAVE True. Room, terrace, tepid soup, beddy-bye.

HENRI Yes, well, you bent your rules a bit last night. What a triumph!

GUSTAVE Thank you.

HENRI Sister Madeleine said to me it was such a shame you became violent . . . argumentative . . . sarcastic . . . spiteful . . . cantankerous . . . evil-minded . . . Because, she said, you were probably a man of some taste and talent.

PHILIPPE I'm wondering if Sister Madeleine isn't a little in love with you, Gustave.

GUSTAVE I should never have biffed her—it's backfired on me.

PHILIPPE Well, so you've met a girl.

HENRI Hardly met . . . encountered.

GUSTAVE What are you going to do about it?

HENRI I don't know . . . nothing.

GUSTAVE Will you go back?

HENRI I might.

GUSTAVE You must.

HENRI What do you want me to do? I'm not going to accost her in the street.

PHILIPPE Why not?

HENRI It isn't done.

PHILIPPE Isn't done? This is 1959, my friend! There's no "isn't done," that's over, gone. You have to get up-to-date with today's woman!

GUSTAVE Right. You have to be modern.

PHILIPPE Make her laugh.

HENRI How am I supposed to make her laugh?

PHILIPPE Tell her a joke.

GUSTAVE A good pun . . . I'll think of one for you.

HENRI No, really, thanks.

GUSTAVE You're right. There's no point in making women laugh.

PHILIPPE Oh, I can't agree. It's essential to make a woman laugh.

GUSTAVE That's a myth—about women going for men who make them laugh. They go for men they fancy. A tall, good-looking, well-built miserable sod with a good head of hair stands a better chance with a woman than a bald midget who's a laugh a minute.

PHILIPPE But between two equally good-looking men, they go for the one who amuses them.

GUSTAVE Take my word for it, I speak from experience, amusing them counts for nothing, they have to fancy you, simple as that.

HENRI (*to Gustave*) Have you ever made a woman laugh?

GUSTAVE I've had them in tears.

PHILIPPE It's a wonderful thing, a woman laughing. They forget themselves, give themselves up, on a plate— personally I think making them laugh is as important as making them climax.

HENRI Both at the same time is difficult.

PHILIPPE I grant you. Unless you're hilarious.

GUSTAVE Never tell a woman that making her laugh and making her climax are equally important. She'll think you're going to divide your concentration and she'll drop you just like that.

HENRI In 1913 when I'd just arrived in Paris I used to follow women in the street.

PHILIPPE Oh yes, very nice.

HENRI But I never plucked up courage to speak to them.

GUSTAVE You should have when the going was good. Now you can't even follow them. Anyway, if women like laughing so much, perhaps you can explain why the vast majority are seen more often than not in the company of humourless creeps.

HENRI For the money!

PHILIPPE Partly for the money and partly because most men are humourless creeps. . . . Look at my sister, married a moron . . .

GUSTAVE I can vouch for that.

HENRI You know his sister?

GUSTAVE She writes to me twice a week.

HENRI So she does.

GUSTAVE . . . Well, what now? You were saying about your sister's moron . . . He's passed out again.

HENRI Give him a shake.

Gustave gets up to shake Philippe, who's starting to come round.

GUSTAVE Oh . . . Philippe, there's a good chap, try not to pass out in the middle of a sentence, it's very annoying.

PHILIPPE (*still out*) . . . We'll take them from the rear, captain . . .

GUSTAVE That's it, you'll take them from the rear . . .

PHILIPPE (*coming to*) Did I have one of my turns? Sorry . . . Are they coming on more frequently . . . ?

HENRI . . . No.

GUSTAVE Not that I've noticed.

PHILIPPE What were we talking about?

HENRI Nothing very exciting.

A pause.

PHILIPPE So . . . you've met a girl.

HENRI We've already done that one, Philippe, but if you insist . . .

PHILIPPE No, no, I get it, it's all coming back, sorry . . . Yes, you have to admit, when it comes to women, we're not exactly spoiled for choice round here.

HENRI The fact that most of them are nuns is a drawback . . . That new little laundress is sweet. You don't think so?

GUSTAVE No, I don't.

HENRI You're very choosy, if you ask me.

GUSTAVE I'm not choosy. Look at her, she's all gums, when she laughs she whinnies, she looks like a horse getting a joke . . . No, the one who's really pretty is one of the cleaning ladies, the big one . . .

They all become thoughtful.

HENRI Ah yes, Marianne . . . Yes, she's nice.

PHILIPPE She has a speech impediment, a slight lisp.

GUSTAVE Does she? . . . I'm not put off.

HENRI No, that doesn't damage the goods.

PHILIPPE I made a pass at her.

HENRI You didn't?

PHILIPPE Did I never tell you?

HENRI No, never.

PHILIPPE Well, I did. I made a pass at her.

GUSTAVE That's it?

PHILIPPE There's not a lot to tell. She was bent over making my bed, I grabbed her arse and said, "Come on, Marianne, give us one" or words to that effect.

HENRI That's not a pass, Philippe, that's what's called attempted rape.

PHILIPPE Where does rape come into it? I didn't do anything, she took off howling "Thithter! Thithter Madeleine! Thave me, thave me!" . . . That's how I know she's got a lisp.

GUSTAVE I thought you were the one for making them laugh.

PHILIPPE Nowadays I have to get a move on, follow me? I faint every five minutes and I've been strongly advised against prolonged exertion.

GUSTAVE I've known the caveman approach to work sometimes.

HENRI I'm more of the courting type.

GUSTAVE Oh, paying court can be delightful too, very nice, but you mustn't overdo it—with women you want, you have to just take them!

HENRI You've had a lot, have you?

GUSTAVE Hundreds!

HENRI Have you ever been married?

GUSTAVE Yes. I got married in 1915!

HENRI And?

GUSTAVE And nothing!

HENRI You're not married any more?

GUSTAVE No, I'm not married anymore. So—what are you going to say to your little girl? Something gallant but leaving no doubt as to the effect she has on you.

PHILIPPE Blow me, there it goes again.

GUSTAVE No, that's a bit obvious.

PHILIPPE No . . . I keep thinking that dog moved.

GUSTAVE Me, too—he's fantastic, you really think he's alive.

HENRI No . . . Philippe actually sees it move.

GUSTAVE Really? You think this dog moves?

PHILIPPE Doesn't it?

HENRI I doubt it. It's made of stone.

PHILIPPE All the same.

GUSTAVE (*to Henri*) Has this sort of thing happened before?

HENRI A few months ago he was sure the terrace was pitching about like a boat . . . and then it passed.

PHILIPPE There, it moved!

GUSTAVE Not a lot though.

PHILIPPE Didn't you see it move?

HENRI Would you like us to remove the dog, Philippe?

PHILIPPE   No, don't bother.

GUSTAVE   Perhaps he'll go off on his own.

HENRI   Give me a hand, Gustave. We'll shift it.

GUSTAVE   Oh no, that would be a shame.

PHILIPPE   Keep your eye on it, we'll all keep our eyes on it, you'll see it move.

They all three stare at the dog.

PHILIPPE *(cont.)* *(after a pause)*   There! What did I tell you?

GUSTAVE   Oh—oh!

HENRI   Give me a hand, Gustave.

GUSTAVE   With your leg you can't do a thing.

HENRI   I'll direct you.

GUSTAVE   How kind.

Gustave moves the statue as best he can; he can hardly move it because it's so heavy.

GUSTAVE *(cont.)*   There, that's moved, Philippe.

PHILIPPE   What did I tell you?

HENRI *(cont.)*   Maybe a bit further.

Gustave pushes the statue further.

HENRI   Is that all right now, Philippe?

PHILIPPE   That's fine. Thank you.

GUSTAVE   You can't hear it either, I trust.

PHILIPPE   Now you're being silly.

GUSTAVE   See those birds, that's moving.

Philippe looks from the birds to the dog and back again.

PHILIPPE   They're migrating birds . . . gathering for the off. I think I need to get up a bit.

GUSTAVE   Go ahead, up you get.

Philippe gets up.

HENRI   Will you be all right?

PHILIPPE   Pitching about a bit, but I'll do. (*He paces.*) So you want us to think of something to say to your girl, is that it?

HENRI   No, I beg you! Anyhow, I must be off.

PHILIPPE   Where?

HENRI   . . . my constitutional.

GUSTAVE   Ah . . . right.

HENRI   What?

GUSTAVE   Nothing. Go for your constitutional.

HENRI   I'm not like you, I need to get out of this place every now and then.

GUSTAVE   With good reason. Go ahead, dear chap.

HENRI   Right, then . . . perhaps see you later.

PHILIPPE   Right then, see you later.

GUSTAVE   Have a nice walk, Henri.

Henri leaves.

GUSTAVE (*cont.*)   Why couldn't he tell us he's off to his girls' school? He's so obvious.

PHILIPPE   There's quite a swell today.

GUSTAVE   I'm telling you, he's stuck on that girl . . . I'm trying to imagine her . . . a tall lissom lily . . .
What's a lily look like?—I've forgotten.

PHILIPPE (*with his hands, he mimes the silhouette of a woman*)
Oh . . . They're a bit like . . . that . . . only, with some . . .

Henri returns.

GUSTAVE   Back already? You see, you can get a move on when you want to.

HENRI   I ran into Mercier. Chassagne's dead!

PHILIPPE   Did Madeleine do it?

HENRI   No, he's killed himself.

BLACKOUT

SCENE 3

Gustave is alone on the terrace. Henri joins him, dressed in mourning black. The dog is back, now facing the poplars, like Gustave.

HENRI   Who put the dog back?

GUSTAVE   I don't know, he must have gone back on his own.

HENRI   Was it you?

GUSTAVE   Of course it was me!

HENRI   You know how it upsets Philippe.

GUSTAVE   I like the dog. He keeps me company.

HENRI   He's looking at the poplars, just like you.

GUSTAVE   Quite. So, how was it?

HENRI   Like a funeral.

GUSTAVE   (*indicating the view*)   Lots of people, I saw . . .

HENRI   Yes, lots. Every veteran who could do the journey was there.

GUSTAVE   I was right not to go. I wouldn't want a crowd of people at my funeral.

HENRI   Oh no?

GUSTAVE   The way I see it, the fewer the mourners, the greater the grief. Was there music?

HENRI   The Funeral March.

GUSTAVE   How original!

HENRI   Well, you have to have it. Military honours.

GUSTAVE   It's very important, the choice of music.

HENRI   What would you like?

GUSTAVE   I love German music, but you don't hear it so much since the war. It's very hard to decide, I'm still thinking about it.

HENRI   Well, don't be overtaken by events.

GUSTAVE   My absence wasn't too noticeable?

HENRI   No.

GUSTAVE   Nobody asked why I wasn't there?

HENRI   No, nobody gave a damn.

GUSTAVE   Good.

HENRI   Gustave, what did you do after the war?

GUSTAVE   Which?

HENRI   The first one, ours.

GUSTAVE   I went home, of course.

HENRI   To your wife?

GUSTAVE   What about my wife?

HENRI   You told me you were married.

GUSTAVE   I must say you're a nosy bugger.

HENRI   Forgive me if I was indiscreet.

GUSTAVE   Don't be such a humbug, that makes it worse. You want to know why I'm not married anymore, is that it?

HENRI   I could care less.

GUSTAVE   Well, I'm going to tell you. My wife left me for an apothecary.

HENRI   That must have been quite a blow.

GUSTAVE   No, it must not "have been quite a blow." In my circle, you know, these things are ordered differently. You wouldn't understand.

HENRI   Your circle?

GUSTAVE   I'm the scion of the highest nobility. One is asked to bear a name . . . my wife proved unworthy of it, that was the hardest thing.

HENRI   Oh, you're an aristocrat. I hadn't realized.

GUSTAVE   One doesn't shout it from the rooftops. What about you? I take it you're a sturdy son of the common people.

HENRI   And proud of it!

GUSTAVE   Have you ever been married?

HENRI   No. After the war I wanted to be a picture-framer.

GUSTAVE   I don't follow.

HENRI   It takes a real artistic touch, you know. You have to choose the right setting. Depending on the subject, the frame has to be narrow and delicate or, as the case may be, more elaborate, heavier . . .

GUSTAVE   Yes, I know what a picture frame is, thank you.

HENRI   I don't know, but I think I would have made a good framer.

GUSTAVE   Why not? I'm sure there are some first-class hopalong picture-framers.

HENRI   Are you cross with me today, or what?

Enter Philippe, his clothes covered in dirt.

GUSTAVE   What happened to you?

HENRI   Are you all right now?

PHILIPPE   Yes, I'm fine . . . That was a bit embarrassing, wasn't it?

HENRI   A bit.

GUSTAVE   What happened?

PHILIPPE   I had one of my turns right by the hole they dug for our friend Chassagne and I fell in.

GUSTAVE   You took his place?

PHILIPPE   In a manner of speaking. I collapsed like a sack into his grave and when I woke up I didn't know where to put myself . . . except, I knew it wasn't where I *had* put myself.

GUSTAVE   I gather my absence was not too noticeable.

PHILIPPE   No.

GUSTAVE   Nobody asked where I was, or why . . .

PHILIPPE   No, nobody gave a damn.

GUSTAVE   Good! You're not bothered that I put the dog back?

PHILIPPE   No, as long as he keeps still.

GUSTAVE   Was Sister Madeleine at the funeral?

HENRI   Not only there but deeply affected.

PHILIPPE   And do you know why?

GUSTAVE   It goes with the job.

PHILIPPE   No, because now he's dead there's no birthday to celebrate. It creates a gap, and she's bloody annoyed.

GUSTAVE   Good!

HENRI   Poor Chassagne . . . It's odd, killing himself like that, at his age . . . I always thought suicide was a young man's game.

GUSTAVE   Like with you—you committed suicide twenty-five years ago.

28

HENRI Please note, Philippe, Gustave is cross with me today.

GUSTAVE (*to Philippe*) No, it's the truth. Twenty-five years in this hole . . .

PHILIPPE Ten years in my case.

GUSTAVE That's different, you're . . . (*Gustave taps his head with his finger.*)

PHILIPPE I'm insane?

GUSTAVE No! But you're seriously in need of medical attention. I'd never stay that long in a home. I need to be . . . where it's all going on.

HENRI For someone who hardly leaves his room, that's a surprise.

PHILIPPE What do you mean, where it's all going on?

HENRI Yes, what have you ever done that's so exciting? Do tell us.

GUSTAVE Oh . . . I wouldn't know where to begin, there's so much.

A beat. Philippe and Henri seem to wait for Gustave's story.

HENRI If there's one thing we're not short of, it's time.

GUSTAVE What would you like me to tell you . . . ? For example, I took part in the Second World War.

PHILIPPE As a soldier? You fought?

GUSTAVE Now you're being silly. But I stayed in Paris during the Occupation. I stuck to my post.

PHILIPPE Meaning what?

GUSTAVE I was face to face with the enemy! I was there!

PHILIPPE That must have put the wind up the Germans.

HENRI They must have thought twice about invading— "Where's that Gustave?"

PHILIPPE When they showed up again in 1940 I would've loved to have given them back their bit of scrap iron. (*He points to his head*.) By the way, how do things stand now, Henri?

HENRI What things?

PHILIPPE Your girl. Have you seen her again?

HENRI I've run across her once or twice. We exchange a friendly hello.

PHILIPPE Hmm . . . progress.

GUSTAVE Can't you get her to come here so we can see what she's like?

HENRI Go and meet your own girls. You'd rather pass the time slapping nuns and staring at poplars.

GUSTAVE She's a little peach ripe for the plucking.

HENRI Look, gentlemen, do me a favour—stop talking about the girl. All right?

The other two nod.

PHILIPPE The next step is to find out her name.

GUSTAVE In his place I'd have sorted it out in two days.

HENRI If you want to see her so much why don't you come with me?

GUSTAVE   Yes, why don't I?

HENRI   So, what are you waiting for?

GUSTAVE   Certainly not for your permission. I'll go if I want.

HENRI   When was the last time you went out?

GUSTAVE   How do I know? The last time . . .

HENRI   Three months ago.

GUSTAVE   There you are—I made a little sortie three months ago.

HENRI   A little sortie? You were found by the gate curled up into a ball and whimpering like a baby. It's true, isn't it, Philippe?

PHILIPPE   Don't make me take sides, I can't stand it.

HENRI   Face up to reality, my friend, the only thing you're capable of is staying slumped on this terrace.

GUSTAVE   What's got into you? Cool down, I'm perfectly capable of getting out of here.

HENRI   No you're not. You're stuck, you're lost without your Sister Madeleine, your dog, your poplars. Even if one could imagine you getting as far as the gate, Sister Madeleine wouldn't let you out.

GUSTAVE   I'd like to see Madeleine stopping me.

HENRI   That's good, because she will.

GUSTAVE (*getting up*)   Very well. In other circumstances, Henri, I could have broken your jaw, but you're old and lame, it wouldn't be a fair fight. I'd rather make you eat your words. Come on, Philippe. Let's go right away!

HENRI With Philippe doesn't count. You have to go on your own.

GUSTAVE . . . fine. I don't need anyone to accompany me.

PHILIPPE Just the same, be careful.

GUSTAVE . . . I'm off!

HENRI Go on, then.

GUSTAVE (*after a pause*) Right. I'm going. Alone. Perhaps I'll see you later. I say perhaps because I'm not sure I'm coming back.

HENRI We'll wait for you here a while and if you don't come back we'll go to dinner without you.

Gustave leaves.

PHILIPPE You may have let the genie out of the bottle

HENRI I'm telling you he won't dare leave.

Henri stands to look further off. Philippe joins him.

PHILIPPE You know, he showed unheard-of courage in the war.

PHILIPPE You know what I miss most here?

HENRI No.

PHILIPPE Music. There's no music around here.

HENRI You like music?

PHILIPPE I studied the piano when I was younger. I even won a gold medal at the Conservatoire . . .

HENRI You never told me you were musical.

PHILIPPE   I was destined for a major career. After the war I wanted to go back to my studies but I tended to pass out every ten minutes . . . which is a handicap for a concert pianist.

HENRI   If it's any consolation, it's a handicap in most jobs.

Pause.

HENRI (*cont.*)   When I was younger I used to play the triangle . . . Maybe we could start a little band, a trio.

PHILIPPE   Don't mention it to Gustave—he'll want to make it a quartet. (*pause*) All quiet. Strange.

GUSTAVE (*emerging from the garden*)   Of course it's all quiet!

HENRI   You gave me a fright. So?

GUSTAVE   So? Just as I might have predicted, Sister Madeleine intercepted me. Incidentally one has to grant that mad doxy a certain courage . . . We stared at each other for a long moment and I said to myself: "Gustave, my son, you've taken part in some of the most murderous campaigns of the Great War, you've lain wounded for three days and nights in a shell crater behind enemy lines, you've collected every medal and decoration the French Army has to offer; you can't beat up a five-foot nun with a runny nose, it's beneath you."

PHILIPPE   Sister Madeleine has a cold?

GUSTAVE   A little one.

HENRI   What did you do?

GUSTAVE   About turn. I came to a decision.

HENRI   So your little stroll wasn't wasted.

GUSTAVE   If we're going to leave, let's do it properly. My proposal is French Indochina!

HENRI   Indochina?

PHILIPPE (*to Henri*)   The genie's out of the bottle.

GUSTAVE   Do you know that part of the world?

PHILIPPE   No.

GUSTAVE   I know it well . . . the Mekong . . . the China Sea . . . monsoons . . . record humidity . . . You've never seen terraces of rice paddies?

Henri and Philippe shake their heads.

GUSTAVE (*cont.*)   Or an old toothless Cambodian fisherman mending his nets? (*same reaction*) Well, you have to see it, my lads, it's another world.

HENRI   I don't doubt it. What would we do in Indochina?

GUSTAVE   What would we do in Indochina? What do we do here?

HENRI   . . . Well . . .

GUSTAVE   You can follow Laotian girls in the street. Laotian girls?

HENRI   I don't know any.

GUSTAVE   You'll learn to know them. Ten thousand years of servitude! For generations, with their little swaddled feet, gliding along straw-covered floors . . . Unable to climax but perfectly submissive. I'm telling you, Indochina is the place for you.

Philippe passes out.

GUSTAVE (*cont.*)   He's passed out again.

HENRI For once with good reason.

Gustave shakes Philippe clumsily.

PHILIPPE We'll take them from the rear, captain, from the rear . . .

Philippe comes round.

GUSTAVE Philippe, you'd better think about having that shrapnel removed.

PHILIPPE Forgive me . . . I left at unable to climax.

GUSTAVE So, what do you say? No more Madeleine, no more tepid soup, no more gloomy funerals—goodbye to all that.

PHILIPPE How do we get to Indochina?

GUSTAVE By boat! Indochina means a boat. Several months at sea. Pretty exciting, eh?

HENRI I don't know if Philippe, in his condition . . .

GUSTAVE Oh, Philippe will be just fine. We'll leave by night, not a word to Madeleine, don't worry about her.

HENRI She's not the problem.

GUSTAVE Thanks to you, Henri—and I'm grateful to you—I came to realise that we can't stay here any longer.

HENRI Yes, but I wasn't thinking of Indochina, I was thinking more of . . . I don't know, going for a picnic.

GUSTAVE A what?

HENRI There's a little clearing on the edge of the village. If you like we could go there and have a picnic.

GUSTAVE A picnic?

HENRI Yes, well, a picnic . . . or something, I don't know . . .

GUSTAVE You're seriously suggesting we go on a picnic?

HENRI How does that strike you, Philippe?

PHILIPPE I don't know . . . It doesn't have the exoticness of Indochina but as an idea I must say it's equally unexpected.

GUSTAVE (*to Philippe*) You're putting Indochina and a picnic on the same level?

PHILIPPE No, I'm just saying both proposals are quite peculiar.

GUSTAVE So, as far as you're concerned, the Indochina peninsula with all its treasures and a picnic in a clearing are the same thing?

HENRI It's not easy to have a discussion with you, Gustave.

GUSTAVE If you want to discuss it, go ahead. I'd just like to say what I think about picnics. Nothing revolts me more than a picnic!

HENRI Fine!

GUSTAVE What is a picnic?

HENRI Let's drop it.

GUSTAVE You set off with a little wicker basket, in which you've put some bread, a bit of sausage and a bottle of milk. You go like a bunch of prats to your little clearing and you spread a mangy blanket to keep your arses dry, and like three old gaffers you stuff yourselves with slices of mortadella, is that it?

HENRI   As you don't want to go on a picnic we don't have to talk about it . . . And besides we're not obliged to do everything together.

GUSTAVE   Yes we are!

HENRI   Why?

GUSTAVE   Because that's the way it is. Because we have no choice.

PHILIPPE   I suggest a compromise.

GUSTAVE   Oh, now we have to compromise.

PHILIPPE   I say we go . . . up there!

HENRI   Where's up there?

PHILIPPE   There. Up that hill, where the poplars are.

GUSTAVE   There where the wind blows. Philippe's got a point, it's not a bad halfway house between Indochina and a picnic.

HENRI   This is not a sane conversation. What would you do with yourself up there?

GUSTAVE   What do you do with yourself down here?

PHILIPPE   What's to stop us, Henri? All right, for some unknown reason you don't understand poplars, that's one thing, but what's to stop us going up there?

HENRI   Nothing . . . nothing except you've got a piece of shrapnel in your skull, and Gustave is clearly deranged— sorry, old chap, I'm just giving you the broad strokes, all right?—apart from that, nothing, these are the only minor obstacles I can see to your little outing.

GUSTAVE   Don't leave out that you limp like a bastard.

PHILIPPE   There where the wind blows, Henri!

GUSTAVE   And let me remind you, a week from now every loony in the place will be coming to chew their cud on our terrace.

PHILIPPE   Think of Madeleine's face!

HENRI   But really, Philippe, remind yourself of the state you're in . . .

GUSTAVE   The wind, Henri, the wind!

HENRI   Yes, right, I've got the symbolism, thanks, very good, beautiful . . .

GUSTAVE   One must strive a little for the epic, old boy.

PHILIPPE   Be epic, Henri! Scale the heights!

HENRI   But I've no desire to be epic. Why do you want me to be epic?

GUSTAVE   The poplars, Henri, the poplars!

HENRI   Oh, to hell with your poplars! I'm going for my constitutional.

He leaves,

GUSTAVE   He's had a thing against those poplars from the start.

PHILIPPE   It's all right, he'll come round if we don't rush him—you have to bear in mind he's not like us, he's not quite right in the head.

BLACKOUT

SCENE 4

Gustave and Henri.

Gustave is unfolding a map. They are watching each other out of the corner of their eye, saying nothing. The stone dog is now by Gustave's chair. Gustave looks from the map to the top of the hill and back. It's not clear whether he is talking to himself, to the dog or to Henri.

GUSTAVE So . . . We're here . . . the poplars are . . . up there . . . Following the road would add at least . . . I'd say sixty kilometres . . . which is stupid. We'll have to cut across. Straight ahead . . . three hundred metres straight up, not impossible.

HENRI He's your pet now, is he?

GUSTAVE Yes, I find him reassuring, and he doesn't interrupt.

HENRI You're not doing a Philippe, are you? You're aware it's a statue?

GUSTAVE Yes, don't worry.

HENRI That's all right, then.

Philippe enters, frantic.

PHILIPPE We have to leave, right away!

GUSTAVE I'm ready.

HENRI What's up?

PHILIPPE You know who's taking Chassagne's place?

HENRI No.

PHILIPPE Teaupin. Lieutenant-Colonel Francois Teaupin. He's arriving this morning.

GUSTAVE I used to know a Teaupin. He was killed in Alsace.

HENRI It's not him.

PHILIPPE No, it's not the same one. And I know this one's birthday. He was born on February 12th!

HENRI So?

PHILIPPE Wake up—February 12th!

HENRI Yes, I heard—that's bad, is it?

PHILIPPE Same as me! We've got the same birthday! You know what that means? Your friend Madeleine has decided to give me the chop. Teaupin'll take the February 12th slot. I'm done for!

HENRI I think you're taking this birthday business a bit too seriously, Philippe.

PHILIPPE Have we ever had two birthday parties on the same day?

HENRI I can't remember.

PHILIPPE Well, we haven't! It's never happened! Do you think it's a coincidence?

HENRI I have a hard time believing that a nun would choose to let the inmates of an old soldiers' home live or die according to what day they were born . . . I could be wrong, but . . .

PHILIPPE You may have a hard time believing it but it's true. A nun who's supposed to have a moral conscience . . . who's allegedly prompted by profoundly charitable instincts . . . has today decided to let me croak. I know Teaupin. A strapping great bruiser. A survivor. I'm out of my class.

GUSTAVE   Maybe we can bump him off.

PHILIPPE   That's a thought.

HENRI   Hang on, hang on, you've gone completely off the rails.

PHILIPPE (*pointing at the dog*)   What's he doing there? Is he following you now?

GUSTAVE   No, it's all right, I put him there.

PHILIPPE   I tell you we have to get out. You could be next on the list!

GUSTAVE   I'm all set. I've studied the map. I'm ready. It's up to Henri.

They look at Henri.

HENRI   Can I think about it?

PHILIPPE   Meanwhile I'm frying on the backburner, is that what you want?

GUSTAVE (*to Henri*)   You heartless bastard.

PHILIPPE   We have to get out *now*.

HENRI   And once up top, what then? We come back?

PHILIPPE   Not on your life!

GUSTAVE   He's got it—this is once and for all.

HENRI (*pause*)   When are we proposing to leave?

GUSTAVE   Right. Let me reveal my plan.

PHILIPPE   I'm listening.

Gustave gets up and faces the poplars.

GUSTAVE   Straight ahead!

PHILIPPE   Great!

HENRI   Straight ahead, straight ahead . . . the cemetery?

GUSTAVE   The poplars.

PHILIPPE   That bitch!

Henri takes the map.

HENRI   Let's have a look at this map. Hang on, I can't see anything, I need my glasses . . . What about this river? How do we get across?

GUSTAVE   Swim.

HENRI   I can't swim, I'm sorry.

GUSTAVE   You're holding us back.

PHILIPPE   Maybe we can wade across.

HENRI   And what if you have one of your turns?

GUSTAVE   What if? What if? What if? With all these conditions, we're better off going, I don't know, on a picnic.

HENRI   . . . We'll have to keep to the road.

PHILIPPE   Fine—keep to the road.

GUSTAVE   No, old boy, you can't go on agreeing with everybody.

HENRI (*holding the map*)   Please, can we try to look at this calmly. Good. We have to start off along this lane, and after four kilometres cut through the wood. That'll save us a good hour. Then we have to get back on this track here . . .

so we can re-victual at Sauzey-le-Potier. It's a detour, I agree, but then we can take this bridge . . . and once we've got across, there are two options: we cut across again, in which case we would have to climb this hill, or . . .

GUSTAVE Are you directing operations now?

HENRI Sorry?

GUSTAVE You're deciding the route and taking over, you've assumed command of the operation.

HENRI No, but I . . .

GUSTAVE Carry on! Carry on, colonel.

HENRI You're getting on my wick, Gustave.

GUSTAVE Sauzey-le-Potier! Why Sauzey-le-Potier? Have you got friends there or what? I don't give a monkeys about Sauzey-le-Potier!

HENRI Nor do I! It's you who wants to go on this excursion! Well, you can go without me.

PHILIPPE Out of the question. You're coming.

GUSTAVE Quite right—the four of us or forget it.

HENRI Four?

GUSTAVE I'm counting the dog.

PHILIPPE We started together on this terrace and we'll finish together under the poplar trees.

GUSTAVE Quite right.

HENRI I'm going mad . . .

GUSTAVE Don't worry about that, you're with us.

HENRI But about the statue.

PHILIPPE That Madeleine bitch!

GUSTAVE (*Gustave snatches the map out of Henri's hands.*) You wet blanket, we're taking you along out of the goodness of our hearts.

PHILIPPE Henri's route seems better to me, Gustave. If we can avoid water courses . . .

GUSTAVE (*with the map*) If you two want to turn this expedition into a constitutional, I'll give way gracefully.

HENRI I'm not even saying we can manage four kilometres on a flat road, never mind the footpath.

GUSTAVE Of course we can . . . Now let's see . . . Next we cross the bridge, it's going well . . . And now this river here . . . we'll have to cross that one, too.

PHILIPPE She's a bitch, that Madeleine.

HENRI (*discouraged*) Yes, we'll have to cross that one, too.

Gustave shows him the map.

GUSTAVE See for yourself, if we take the road we'll be following the river practically all around the department . . . That'll take three months. You will have to go to Sauzey-le-Potier another time.

HENRI A raft!

GUSTAVE (*after some thought*) Wait! I'll take you across on my back.

PHILIPPE What?

GUSTAVE It's not much of a river, at this time of year you can walk it. I'll carry you, one at a time.

Gustave crouches down in front of Philippe.

GUSTAVE (*cont.*) Go on, give it a try, climb on my back.

PHILIPPE Are you sure about this?

GUSTAVE Climb up, I'm telling you.

Philippe puts his legs around Gustave and clings to his neck.

PHILIPPE Like this?

GUSTAVE You're choking me . . . That's better.

PHILIPPE I don't find this position very natural.

GUSTAVE Nor do I. Now faint, just to see.

PHILIPPE You want me to faint?

GUSTAVE Pretend.

PHILIPPE I like to make the most of my periods of lucidity, but if you insist . . .

Philippe pretends to faint.

GUSTAVE (*at the point of apoplexy from the weight*) There . . . you see! (*to Henri*) What do you say?

HENRI I'm not saying a thing.

GUSTAVE (*to Philippe*) That's fine . . . that's fine. Philippe, you can get off . . . Philippe?

HENRI He's passed out.

GUSTAVE (*tottering*) Shit, he's a weight.

HENRI Let me help you.

45

GUSTAVE (*hoping to wake him up*)   From the rear, captain . . .

PHILIPPE   No, no, I'm all right. I was having you on.

Philippe gets down. Gustave straightens.

GUSTAVE (*to Henri*)   Now you.

HENRI   What?

GUSTAVE   Your turn. Climb up. You can't swim, I'm sure to have to carry you.

HENRI   No, I can wade. You're right, at this time of year the water will be shallow.

GUSTAVE   You're quite sure?

HENRI   Quite sure.

GUSTAVE   I mean, I've never abandoned a wounded man. I can easily . . .

He offers his back.

HENRI   It'll be fine, don't worry.

GUSTAVE (*his back hurting*)   Good. That's one problem out of the way.

HENRI   Wouldn't it be simpler if we roped up?

PHILIPPE   We'd need a rope.

HENRI   True, that would be indispensable.

He finds a length of hose.

HENRI (*cont.*)   Voila!

GUSTAVE   Let's have a look.

Gustave takes the hose and examines it closely.

GUSTAVE (*cont.*)   It's a hose!

HENRI   I know.

GUSTAVE (*He pulls on it.*)   It'll do.

He returns it to Henri.

HENRI   So . . . what we have to do is rope ourselves up for
the steeper bits in case one of us stumbles or falls. A three
hundred metre climb is no joke. Let's have a go. Over here,
Philippe. It mustn't be too short or too long . . . Now you,
Gustave.

GUSTAVE   I should be leading, but still . . .

HENRI   This is just to try, you'll be leading, with Philippe in
the middle.

PHILIPPE   I go in the middle?

HENRI   No, not for the moment, put yourself at the other
end, it's a trial run . . . You make a knot like this . . .

GUSTAVE   Have you done some mountaineering?

HENRI   As a young man.

GUSTAVE   That was a long time ago.

*Henri demonstrates the knot. Philippe takes the other end and does
the same. Gustave is in the middle, holding the rope.*

GUSTAVE (*cont.*)   And I'll stay here like an arse, holding the
rope so he can . . .

PHILIPPE   But I've just managed to do my knot.

HENRI   It doesn't matter, you can do it again.

*Philippe unties himself. Gustave takes the end of the rope and ties it
round himself.*

GUSTAVE (*to himself*) Absurd . . . I should be in the lead . . .

HENRI You will be in the lead! I'm showing you, it's a trial go! (*Henri shows him.*) Rope up like this . . . there . . . and pass the end of the rope . . . like this . . . there you are!

GUSTAVE (*still to himself*) I know, I know, but I don't give a damn, I'm going to be leader.

HENRI Dammit, Gustave! I'm showing you, that's all!

GUSTAVE Yes, all right, apologies, go on. I can see roping up is your thing, I'm putting you in command.

Gustave is roped up.

HENRI And now you, Philippe.

Philippe takes the rope to redo his knot.

GUSTAVE (*to Philippe*) I hope you saw how I did mine, because you'll be in the middle.

PHILIPPE Shut up a minute, I'm trying to do my knot.

HENRI (*to Philippe*) Here!— Put the end back through the loop . . . Very good. There, we're roped up!

GUSTAVE Yes, so long as we agree it doesn't mean a thing, because Philippe will be in the middle and I'll be leading.

HENRI Yes! Yes! You'll be leading, Philippe in the middle and me at the end. Happy now?

GUSTAVE Ooooh . . . this expedition is making you jittery, isn't it?

PHILIPPE . . . Sorry, I have to sit down a minute . . .

Philippe collapses on his chair, causing the others to do the same. They rest quietly in their usual places, roped together.

GUSTAVE We'll need provisions, of course.

PHILIPPE How many days' march, do you reckon?

GUSTAVE Two, possibly three. (*to Henri*) I suggest you be responsible for provisions.

HENRI Why me?

GUSTAVE You're the picnic specialist.

PHILIPPE Blankets, remember to take blankets.

GUSTAVE Good. So, when do we set off?

PHILIPPE Time to organise things . . . I don't know. In three days, the 18th.

GUSTAVE We must leave at night.

HENRI Why at night?

PHILIPPE Yes, why at night?

GUSTAVE To make sure we don't meet anyone.

PHILIPPE We're not going to meet many people if we're going cross-country.

GUSTAVE No, but leaving the grounds . . . on the road.

PHILIPPE At dawn, then. We'll leave at dawn.

GUSTAVE At dawn! Good! I like that.

HENRI Ideal.

PHILIPPE If only I'd stayed put at my sister's, I wouldn't be in this desperate situation.

HENRI Why didn't you?

GUSTAVE You don't know his sister!

PHILIPPE   No! It's my brother-in-law. What a moron. I ended up having to pretend to faint into my plate so I wouldn't have to listen to him. So I opted to come here.

GUSTAVE   You were quite right!

PHILIPPE   Except now they're going to let me die like a down-and-out.

HENRI   Nobody's going to let you die, Philippe.

GUSTAVE   Of course not.

Philippe passes out.

HENRI   Out again!

GUSTAVE   He can't come to any harm, he's roped up.

PHILIPPE   From the rear, captain, we'll take them from the rear.

GUSTAVE   Here he comes.

PHILIPPE (*recovering*)   Sorry. You have to agree, it's happening more and more often.

GUSTAVE   I haven't noticed!

HENRI   No . . . It's more often but not more and more often.

GUSTAVE   Why do you always say "We'll take them from the rear, captain" when you're coming round?

HENRI   A memory from the war . . .

PHILIPPE   Oh, do I say that? I'm not aware of it.

GUSTAVE   Who was this captain?

PHILIPPE   Ah, she was gorgeous . . . a big woman, with remarkable breasts, like a couple of howitzers.

HENRI An artillery captain?

PHILIPPE No, no, a dressmaker from Maubeuge. I used to look her up on leave. She liked me to call her captain, it excited her. We had some great times, she and I . . .

HENRI (*trying to understand*) But why would you say to her "We'll take them from the rear, captain"?

Gustave and Philippe are surprised by the question.

GUSTAVE Oh, honestly, Henri!

HENRI (*catching up*) Oh, sorry, sorry . . . yes, quite.

PHILIPPE Well, good. I'm going to lie low in my room. I get the feeling Madeleine is looking for me. How do I untie this knot?

HENRI Pull on the little end, Philippe!

He unties the knot; Philippe sets off.

HENRI (*cont.*) See you at dinner. We'll talk some more.

Gustave seems to make sure Philippe has left.

GUSTAVE He's had it.

HENRI A goner!

GUSTAVE And there's his little habit of asking if it's getting more frequent.

HENRI One day he'll leave us just like that, in the middle of a sentence. He'll go off on a comma. I'm only going up there with you for his sake.

GUSTAVE Tell me, Henri, when you go out in the road for your stroll . . .

HENRI Yes . . . I'm just off, incidentally.

GUSTAVE Do you meet people?

HENRI You want to know if I meet people in the street? Sometimes, yes.

GUSTAVE And what . . . I mean, what do you do?

HENRI I greet them . . . yes, I often give them a little nod.

GUSTAVE Yes, I see. How do you mean? A little nod of the head . . . like this?

HENRI Yes, like that, no more, just a little nod.

GUSTAVE And they don't speak to you? They don't say a word?

HENRI Rarely, very rarely.

GUSTAVE Ah . . . good . . . good. Because, as we were mentioning the other day, it's a long time since I went out, and I was wondering if things had changed much.

HENRI No, they're just the same, a little nod or a word. It's not the kind of thing that changes much, you know.

Gustave appears to practise a nod.

HENRI *(cont.)* What are you doing? Are you practising?

GUSTAVE Meet me!

HENRI What?

GUSTAVE We don't know each other, we pretend to pass in the street by chance, go on.

HENRI If you like.

Henri retreats and comes back towards Gustave. Gustave seems to be getting his nod ready.

GUSTAVE Right!

HENRI (*drawing level with Gustave*) Ah, Gustave!—you old
rogue! How's tricks? We were just talking about you. I
haven't seen you for ages. Family all right? What's become
of you?

*Gustave starts to shake. Henri, pleased with his trick, laughs, then
realises he's been cruel.*

HENRI (*cont.*) Tell you what. Would you like to try going
out, the two of us? I'll come with you. It's the time of day
when we might see my little schoolteacher.

BLACKOUT

SCENE 5

*Gustave and Philippe. Gustave has a pair of binoculars around his
neck.*

GUSTAVE A very attractive young woman!

PHILIPPE Oh, yes?

GUSTAVE A little darling.

PHILIPPE Did you speak to her?

GUSTAVE No. I gave her a little nod, like this.

PHILIPPE Like what?

GUSTAVE Like this.

He does the nod.

PHILIPPE Bravo. Well done. I'm proud of you, Gustave.
You got a grip on yourself, you went out into the village,
that's terrific. I'm very pleased with you.

53

GUSTAVE (*looking at the poplars through his binoculars*)   Won't be long before we're up there.

PHILIPPE   May I?

Gustave passes him the binoculars.

PHILIPPE (*cont.*)   Ah . . . there they are . . . swaying away . . .

GUSTAVE   Where's Henri?

PHILIPPE   I asked him to go and sound out Madeleine about what sort of shape Teaupin's in. He could have a malignant disease.

GUSTAVE   So you're counting on the competition wasting away.

PHILIPPE (*bringing out a notebook*)   I've started a journal, a sort of log.

GUSTAVE   Great idea.

PHILIPPE   I'm calling it "The Wind in the Poplars, or Three Crocks on Campaign."

GUSTAVE   Speak for yourselves.

PHILIPPE   "Two Crocks and a Crackpot." Fine, the title's not important. My idea is we take turns writing down our thoughts and impressions.

Henri enters.

HENRI   I've found some first-rate blankets.

He puts down the blankets.

GUSTAVE   Let's have a look.

HENRI   Warm but light.

GUSTAVE Just the job.

PHILIPPE Any news of Teaupin?

HENRI Yes . . . all I can tell you is . . . Teaupin is not, shall we say, on his way out.

PHILIPPE He's fighting fit.

HENRI Fighting fit! (*to make Philippe feel better*) These are some blankets! By the way, you know about our Gustave? Fantastic, eh? He went out normal as you like—we did the cemetery.

GUSTAVE Since when was I "your Gustave"—stop talking about me as if I'm a child.

PHILIPPE I've started a log, Henri. We can each put down our thoughts and impressions.

HENRI You can start by recording that I've found some first-rate blankets. We're lucky it's August, but the nights get chilly.

Henri folds the blanket with great care. The other two watch him for a while.

GUSTAVE What are you doing?

HENRI I like to get the creases right.

GUSTAVE Make an entry in the log, Philippe. "Tuesday, August 16th. Henri applies particular care to the folding of the blankets."

HENRI An officer who's been decorated as often as you should know that a good soldier's kit is always immaculate. (*He finishes folding.*) There.

PHILIPPE That's very good.

HENRI   The important thing is not to load ourselves down. Remember, travel light. A small haversack each, and one large bag we'll take turns to carry, Gustave and me . . . mostly Gustave.

GUSTAVE (*to Philippe*)   He didn't want to go and now he's putting himself in charge, he's taking over.

HENRI   All subject to your approval.

GUSTAVE   Carry on! (*pointing to the binoculars*) Seen these?

HENRI   Binoculars!—good.

GUSTAVE   You didn't think of that, did you? Do you want to try them?

Henri looks through the binoculars.

HENRI   Ah, yes . . . You can almost read the inscriptions . . .

PHILIPPE   The advance is settled for the 18th. Agreed?

HENRI   Yes, assuming no hold-ups.

GUSTAVE   What about the weather forecast? Do we have any info?

HENRI   No, not exactly.

GUSTAVE   Can't you tell with your leg?

HENRI   No. How would I tell with my leg?

GUSTAVE   Old people often have pains, rheumatism and so on, which flare up when it's going to rain.

HENRI   Well, you should know.

PHILIPPE (*giving the log to Gustave*)   Gustave, here—you may want to put some thoughts down before we set off.

GUSTAVE Delighted. Oh, you've already started. May I read?

PHILIPPE Of course—it's a collective work.

GUSTAVE "Tuesday, August 16th, nine a.m. Despite the dread this expedition instils in me, I rejoice to be setting off with my comrades. Will my physical condition let me reach our objective? That's the only question. The fact is I'm not tip-top. I haven't had an erection worthy of the name for six months. That's a sign."

HENRI So it's a log you put everything in.

PHILIPPE One can't start off keeping things back.

HENRI No, indeed.

GUSTAVE He's right—it's a sign. (*solemn and troubled*) Six months!

HENRI Worthy of the name, that's exactly it, "worthy of the name."

PHILIPPE All the same I'm not past it yet!

GUSTAVE (*indicating Philippe and himself*) Not us, no, but we must keep on our toes. We should exercise.

Gustave gets up and starts doing gymnastics.

GUSTAVE (*cont.*) Mens sana in corpore sano. Do what I do.

The other two comply.

HENRI Is this really necessary?

GUSTAVE Essential. We're rusty, old boy. Go on, bend down and touch your toes.

The other two comply.

57

GUSTAVE (*cont.*)   Take deep breaths.

After a moment, Philippe faints.

GUSTAVE (*cont.*)   Nothing serious, carry on, he'll catch up!

Henri hesitates but finally helps Philippe to his chair. Gustave continues on his own.

PHILIPPE   From the rear, captain . . .

HENRI   You could have a problem there.

GUSTAVE (*still at it*)   Nothing to it.

PHILIPPE (*coming round*)   Thanks . . . It's true I need to exercise but very, very gently.

HENRI   There you are, sit yourself down.

GUSTAVE (*doing well*)   I feel better already. We'll be on the summit in no time. We're Crusaders, gentlemen, straight for the poplars with sabres drawn, and anyone who's in the way gets it in the neck. You'll see how great you'll feel on the top. (*He addresses the dog.*) Isn't that right? A change of air is what you need. (*He pats the dog's flank.*) He'll outlive us all!

HENRI   No doubt about that.

GUSTAVE   It'll be great to see him up there. It's where he belongs.

HENRI   All the same, you're not seriously thinking of bringing him?

GUSTAVE   We can't possibly leave this dog behind.

HENRI   You're joking. (*to Philippe*) Tell me he's joking.

PHILIPPE   He's not joking.

GUSTAVE Have you got something against dogs?

HENRI No. Only against lugging around two-hundred-pound stone statues of dogs.

GUSTAVE And that's your only objection? That he's made of stone?

HENRI Yes. That's the only thing I've got against him.

GUSTAVE Well, at least your frankness does you credit.

HENRI The way your mind works, Gustave, doesn't bear thinking about. You're really counting on taking the dog?

GUSTAVE I'm taking the dog!

HENRI (*to Philippe*) Did you know he wanted to take the dog?

PHILIPPE I had an awful feeling about it.

GUSTAVE I'm taking the dog!

HENRI Don't abandon me, Philippe. Say something.

PHILIPPE Well, I often see the dog move . . . so it's difficult to take sides.

HENRI But you're aware, aren't you, that bringing the dog would strangely complicate the operation, yes or no?

GUSTAVE "Complicate the operation" . . . Since when are you afraid of complication? Everything is complicated to us, every single thing. Finding a good reason to get up in the morning is infinitely more complicated than transporting this dog whose place is up there, with us.

PHILIPPE Perhaps we could . . . maybe there's a way of . . .

HENRI   No, there's no way . . . I know you think it'll trot after us but you need help, my friend, it's made of stone.

GUSTAVE   You're missing the point, Henri. For you this is a stroll in the country among friends. Imagine we're commandos whose mission is to escape from this terrace. Think about it, Henri—we're going to escape!

HENRI   With escapes, one avoids loading oneself down with nonessentials.

PHILIPPE   What about putting it on a plank, on wheels? Like a field gun.

HENRI   And who's going to pull it?

PHILIPPE   Gustave! It's his dog.

GUSTAVE   Of course. Good idea.

HENRI   This is ridiculous!

GUSTAVE   (*to Henri*)   Should I tell you something? I get the feeling you've never believed in this.

HENRI   How could anyone believe in it?

GUSTAVE   You haven't got the soul of a Crusader.

HENRI   Like you, you mean? Some Crusader you make! You go down the road with me and when we see that young woman, you give her a little nod, like this, at thirty metres . . . when she's not even looking.

GUSTAVE   That's the nod one gives in these cases. (*to Philippe*) It was him who told me, Philippe.

PHILIPPE   Don't drag me into it, please.

HENRI   You've gone mad.

GUSTAVE It's not exactly sane to get so worked up about a dog.

HENRI A two-hundred-pound unshiftable dog.

GUSTAVE You give up at the least difficulty.

HENRI You're right. My heart was never in it. I was just trying to relieve the boredom for a moment. I'm sorry.

PHILIPPE Henri, please, let's have a think. Here's the situation: I'm not well, Gustave is tolerably deranged, the dog weighs a ton, and we've a long way to go . . .

GUSTAVE You forgot to mention that Henri is lame.

PHILIPPE And you're lame. Good! So . . . where's the problem? What's to stop us at least having a go? Think of Madeleine's face!

GUSTAVE That's true! Especially when she realises we've pinched her dog!

HENRI I know damn well what we'll find when we get up there. An uncomfortable windy hilltop, and beyond it at best, a little valley strangely similar to the one we just left, only further off, much further, with the chance of another refuge rather like this one, which might have the goodness to take us in . . . another terrace . . . another cemetery . . . nothing changes, except . . . one day . . . quite soon, it won't be three Crusaders anymore, it'll be two . . . then one . . . and finally just a dog on a different terrace. (*long pause*) No. You're right, Gustave. I'd make a sorry Crusader . . . I'll have to take back my blanket.

GUSTAVE You're giving up?

HENRI Obviously.

GUSTAVE No appeal? You're resigning from the commando?

HENRI I'm resigning.

GUSTAVE I'm disappointed in you . . . very disappointed.

PHILIPPE (*gesturing at the dog*) And so's he.

Henri starts to go.

GUSTAVE You're leaving right now?

HENRI Yes.

GUSTAVE We're in the middle of a confab.

HENRI It seems to me the confab is over.

PHILIPPE So—it's you or the dog.

HENRI No, in no case is it me, I can hardly make it plainer.

GUSTAVE Fine!

HENRI So . . . bon voyage, and good luck!

Henri leaves.

GUSTAVE Never trust a man who doesn't like dogs.

BLACKOUT

SCENE 6

Gustave, Henri and Philippe.

GUSTAVE The lovely colours of autumn.

PHILIPPE I saw Teaupin. You know what he was doing?
Press-ups! He's jeering at me. There he was with his ugly
mug like a boiled rat, glad to be alive. When he sees me, he

puts on speed, deep breaths, muscles rippling . . . My chances of survival are decreasing by the minute.

GUSTAVE Can't you talk about something else?

PHILIPPE Like what?

HENRI Cycling . . .

PHILIPPE Teaupin used to be a champion cyclist?

HENRI Not cycling.

GUSTAVE Cycling is all about stamina.

PHILIPPE Just my luck. I've been thinking about how to do away with him.

GUSTAVE You'd like to eliminate Teaupin physically?

PHILIPPE Yes . . . but I need your help. Teaupin's taken to doing his exercises below the other terrace.

GUSTAVE Oh, yes.

PHILIPPE Well, you know that big cast iron basin up on the edge?

GUSTAVE I know it.

PHILIPPE Well, we could tip it over. It would fall "accidentally" on Teaupin while he's doing his press-ups. What they don't see they don't know.

GUSTAVE But that basin's enormous.

PHILIPPE There's where you come in.

HENRI Yes, you're the specialist on moving heavy objects.

PHILIPPE (*to Gustave*) So, what do you say?

GUSTAVE   What do I say . . . what do I say . . . ? I'm not against doing away with Teaupin . . . Although there's always some moralistic prig who'll object. (*beat*) Aren't you afraid Teaupin may be easily replaced? There must be a whole bunch of chaps born on February 12th.

PHILIPPE   We'll get rid of the lot of them one by one!

GUSTAVE   Sooner or later someone's bound to notice.

PHILIPPE   In that case, we'll get together all the veterans born on February 12th and blow them sky high in one go.

GUSTAVE   That would require considerable organisation.

PHILIPPE   Then it's us who'll have to go. We'll all go to my sister's.

HENRI   I thought your sister's was unendurable.

PHILIPPE   Yes, but with the three of us we would neutralize the brother-in-law.

HENRI   Surely the solution is to send Teaupin to your sister's on his own.

GUSTAVE   To your sister's isn't possible.

PHILIPPE   Why?

HENRI (*to Gustave*)   You mean because it would put her out?

PHILIPPE   She's still my sister, and since it's a matter of life and death . . .

GUSTAVE   No, but to your sister's—I'm telling you, you can't.

PHILIPPE   On the contrary, it's an excellent idea.

HENRI   Is it far?

GUSTAVE Further than you think.

PHILIPPE No it's not! You were ready to go to Indochina. I'm going to write to her to set it up.

GUSTAVE Nobody can go to your sister's, Philippe!

PHILIPPE I should like to know why not.

GUSTAVE Because she's dead.

PHILIPPE She's dead?

GUSTAVE Yes.

PHILIPPE Since when?

GUSTAVE A month ago . . . I'm sorry.

PHILIPPE You could have told me.

GUSTAVE I . . . I was going to . . . and then . . .

HENRI Excuse me, Philippe, but if you read your post . . .

PHILIPPE Denise is dead.

GUSTAVE Don't worry, I took care of the funeral arrangements.

PHILIPPE . . . Thank you.

GUSTAVE I believe it went well. It wasn't easy organising everything at long distance.

PHILIPPE Really?

GUSTAVE In as much as I didn't see eye to eye with your family about the inscription on the gravestone. Your brother-in-law suggested: "In memory of our adored and beloved Denise" . . . Hopeless! There's something tautological about "adored and beloved." If she's adored she's beloved, right?

PHILIPPE   She was.

GUSTAVE   There you are, I knew you'd agree. Well, there was no way to reason with him. I suggested, "Our dear Denise," full stop. I always incline to understatement. Well, he didn't want to know.

PHILIPPE   He's a moron, I told you.

GUSTAVE   Your whole family is pig-headed!

HENRI   What was the inscription in the end?

GUSTAVE   I don't know. I'm not on speaking terms with any of them. By the way, this may not be the moment but I had to pay for a few things . . .

PHILIPPE   Yes . . . let me know . . . So Denise is dead.

GUSTAVE   Yes.

Silence. Philippe takes the journal and hands it to Henri.

PHILIPPE   Perhaps we should make an entry in the log . . . Here, Henri, you haven't written anything yet.

HENRI   But . . . I didn't know her.

GUSTAVE   We've all written something.

HENRI (*indicating the dog*)   Even him?

GUSTAVE   Even him.

Intrigued despite himself, Henri takes the journal.

HENRI   It doesn't go beyond August 18th . . .

GUSTAVE (*accusing*)   And why do you think that is?

HENRI (*reads*)   "August 18th. Dawn. The moment of decision has arrived. One of the members of the commando has refused to leave his terrace, thus combining treason with cowardice. His lack of moral fibre has utterly compromised our expedition. The three of us who are left . . . (*beat*) Our leader Gustave, his second-in-command Philippe and I . . . (*Henri glances at the dog.*) and I . . . are forced to give up our heroic enterprise, leaving Phillippe at the mercy of the murderous folly of Sister Madeleine. Should the traitor presume to join us on our terrace I intend to make my feelings plain by ignoring him completely." Have you got a pencil?

GUSTAVE   Here.

Henri writes, then hands the journal to Gustave.

PHILIPPE   What's he written?

GUSTAVE (*He reads.*)   "September 20th. You're all barking. Except the dog."

Pause.

GUSTAVE (*cont.*)   Oh, look up there—aren't they beautiful?

HENRI   What?

GUSTAVE   The geese, flying in V formation.

PHILIPPE   They're off! Heading south to . . . to the mating grounds.

GUSTAVE   Trollops!

HENRI   Where? Have you got your binoculars by any chance?

GUSTAVE   No.

PHILIPPE Do you know why they fly in V formation?

HENRI No.

PHILIPPE The one in front parts the air, so the others don't get too tired. During the whole length of their journey they take turns to lead the flock.

Philippe gets up and holds out his arms like wings. He is soon joined by Gustave, who takes his place in front.

HENRI Is that true?

PHILIPPE Yes . . . they're geese.

Henri takes his place. They form a V.

HENRI I can't see them.

GUSTAVE They're just above the poplars.

PHILIPPE Can you see the poplars?

GUSTAVE They're just above.

HENRI No . . . Oh yes . . . now I see them.

They are now ready to "take off."

BLACKOUT.

THE END

Gérald Sibleyras was born in Paris in 1961. *Heroes*, or *Le Vent des Peupliers*, was originally commissioned by Théâtre Montparnasse and received four Molière nominations in 2003. His other plays include *Le Béret de la Torture*, which he cowrote with Jean Dell, and *Un Petit Jeu sans Conséquence*, which received five Molière awards in 2003. His most recent play, *Une Huere et Demie de Retard* (again cowritten with Dell), premiered at Théâtre des Mathurins. Currently he is working on two plays, *La Danse de l'Albatros* and *Vive Bouchon!*

Tom Stoppard's plays include *Rosencrantz and Guildenstern Are Dead*, *The Real Inspector Hound*, *Enter a Free Man*, *Albert's Bridge*, *After Magritte*, *Travesties*, *Dirty Linen*, *Jumpers*, *New-Found-Land*, *Night and Day*, *The Real Thing*, *Hapgood*, *Artist Descending a Staircase*, *Every Good Boy Deserves Favour*, *Arcadia*, *The Invention of Love*, *The Coast of Utopia (Voyage, Shipwreck* and *Salvage)* and *Rock 'n' Roll*.